Loaders

by Charles Lennie

ABDO
CONSTRUCTION MACHINES
Kids

www.abdopublishing.com

Published by Abdo Kids, a division of ABDO, P.O. Box 398166, Minneapolis, Minnesota 55439.

Copyright © 2015 by Abdo Consulting Group, Inc. International copyrights reserved in all countries. No part of this book may be reproduced in any form without written permission from the publisher.

Printed in the United States of America, North Mankato, Minnesota.

052014

092014

 THIS BOOK CONTAINS
RECYCLED MATERIALS

Photo Credits: Shutterstock, Thinkstock

Production Contributors: Teddy Borth, Jennie Forsberg, Grace Hansen

Design Contributors: Candice Keimig, Laura Rask, Dorothy Toth

Library of Congress Control Number: 2013952543

Cataloging-in-Publication Data

Lennie, Charles.

 Loaders / Charles Lennie.

  p. cm. -- (Construction machines)

ISBN 978-1-62970-020-5 (lib. bdg.)

Includes bibliographical references and index.

1. Loaders (Machines)--Juvenile literature. 2. Excavation--Juvenile literature. 3. Construction equipment--Juvenile literature.   I. Title.

621.8--dc23

                    2013952543

Table of Contents

Loaders

Loaders are used every
day. They are often used
at construction sites.

4

A loader lifts and moves **material**. It can move dirt, snow, rocks, and more.

6

A loader helps move building **material** too. It can move brick and metal.

A loader can help with cleanup. It fills dump trucks with **waste**. The dump truck carries the waste away.

11

Loader Parts

A loader has a few main parts.

The driver sits in the **cab**.

The engine is behind the cab.

cab

engine

13

Two arms move up and down. They hold the bucket. The bucket holds the **material**.

15

Most loaders move
on wheels. Others
move on **tracks**.

17

Different Kinds

There are small loaders. They sometimes have **backhoes**. Backhoes help to dig.

19

There are very big loaders.

They can move a lot of material!

21

More Facts

- If you live in a place that snows, you might see a loader helping with snow removal.

- Farmers use tractor loaders. Tractor loaders can help with many tasks on the farm.

- Some loaders have claws in place of buckets. They help move things like large logs at sawmills.

22

Glossary

backhoe – a machine with a bucket that is used for digging.

cab – where the driver sits to control the machine.

material – anything used for construction, or making something else.

track – continuous metal band around the wheels of a heavy vehicle.

waste – material that is no longer useful.

Index

abdokids.com

Use this code to log on to abdokids.com and access crafts, games, videos and more!

Abdo Kids Code:
CLK0205